THIS WALKER BOOK BELONGS TO:

For Josie

First published 1993 by
Walker Books Ltd
87 Vauxhall Walk
London SE11 5HJ

This edition published 1995

10 9

© 1993 Lucy Cousins

This book has been typeset in Palatino
with Tiepolo punctuation.

Printed in Hong Kong

British Library Cataloguing in Publication Data
A catalogue record for this book is
available from the British Library.

ISBN 0-7445-3672-3

Noah's Ark

Retold and illustrated by

Lucy Cousins

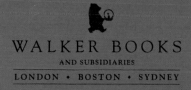

WALKER BOOKS
AND SUBSIDIARIES
LONDON · BOSTON · SYDNEY

A long time ago there lived
a man called Noah.
Noah was a good man,
who trusted in God.

There were also many wicked people in the world. God wanted to punish the wicked people, so he said to Noah...

"I shall make
and wash all
Build an
and all

a flood of water

the wicked people away.

ark for your family

the animals."

Noah worked   for years

and years   and years ...

to build the ark.

At last the ark was finished.

Noah and his family gathered lots of food.

Then the animals came,
two by two...

two by two...

into the ark.

When the ark was full
Noah felt a drop of rain.

It rained

and rained

and rained.

It rained ...

for forty days and forty nights.

The world was covered
with water.

At last the rain stopped
and the sun came out.
Noah sent a dove to
find dry land.

The dove came back with
a leafy twig.
"Hurrah!" shouted Noah.
"The flood has ended."

But many more days passed
before the ark came to rest
on dry land.

Then Noah and all
the animals came
safely out of
the ark...

and life began again on the earth.

MORE WALKER PAPERBACKS
For You to Enjoy

BIBLE STORIES
by Marcia Williams

"Highly recommended for 4-year-olds upwards,
these colourful books retell exciting Old Testament stories
as if they happened yesterday. Lively and attractive illustrations feature
comic-style bubbles above simple texts." *Parents*

0-7445-6058-6   *The Amazing Story of Noah's Ark*
0-7445-6060-8   *Joseph and His Magnificent Coat of Many Colours*
0-7445-6059-4   *Jonah and the Whale*

£4.99 each

THE NATIVITY
by Juan Wijngaard

"A real treasure… Lovely to read out loud and accompanied
by illustrations of beauty." *The Daily Mail*

0-7445-2039-8   £5.99

THE TALE OF TOBIAS
retold by Jan Mark, illustrated by Rachel Merriman

A man and his dog take a journey in the company of a stranger who turns out to be an angel
in this entertaining tale taken from the Apocrypha, a collection of Biblical books.

"A wonderful retelling of a Biblical story." *Sunday Telegraph*

0-7445-4769-5   £4.99

Walker Paperbacks are available from most booksellers, or by post from B.B.C.S., P.O. Box 941, Hull, North Humberside HU1 3YQ

24 hour telephone credit card line 01482 224626

To order, send: Title, author, ISBN number and price for each book ordered, your full name and address,
cheque or postal order payable to BBCS for the total amount and allow the following for postage and packing:
UK and BFPO: £1.00 for the first book, and 50p for each additional book to a maximum of £3.50.
Overseas and Eire: £2.00 for the first book, £1.00 for the second and 50p for each additional book.

Prices and availability are subject to change without notice.